HOW THINGS WORK

WICKED
WHEELS

carbon

Boardman

p

This is a Parragon Book
This edition published in 2001

Parragon
Queen Street House
4 Queen Street
Bath BA1 1HE, UK

ISBN 0-75255-297-X

Printed in Dubai, U.A.E.

Produced by
Monkey Puzzle Media Ltd
Gissing's Farm
Fressingfield
Suffolk IP21 5SH
UK

Designer: Tim Mayer
Cover design: David West Children's Books
Editor: Linda Sonntag
Editorial assistance: Lynda Lines and Jenny Siklós
Indexer: Caroline Hamilton
Project manager: Katie Orchard

CONTENTS

SPEED BIKE

No frame tubes
The frame is one piece of moulded material called carbon fibre composite. It is extremely light and strong, shaped to withstand all the main stresses put on it without any excess material or extra weight.

No freewheel
If you stop pedalling on a sprint or speed bike, the pedals keep turning. There is no freewheel, as on a normal bike, that allows the pedals to stay still while the bicycle rolls along.

ON THE ROAD
Speed bicycles are too specialized to ride on roads. The basic design of the road racer or touring bike, with its down-curved drop-handlebars, has not changed for more than 50 years.

No spokes
As a spoke moves through the air, both turning with the wheel and moving forward with it, this creates air resistance or friction. The solid spokeless wheel cuts out the air friction of the 30–40 normal spokes.

No air-filled tyres
A cycle track is very flat, without lumps and bumps. So the speed or sprint bike needs only thin, solid rubber treads.

No left stays
The back wheel is fixed to one side of the frame, like the front wheel and for the same reason.

No pedal clips
Expert cyclists pull the pedal up as well as push it down, for greater power and speed. Older style pedals had clips and straps that fitted around a cycling shoe. Newer ones have clips that attach to clips on the soles of the shoes, similar to ski bindings that clip ski boots to skis.

BICYCLE SPEEDS
In a road race a cyclist needs air-filled tyres to iron out bumps in the road, gears to cope with the ups and downs of hills and brakes to manoeuvre between competitors or avoid obstacles. But a cycle track is smooth and banked, usually indoors, empty apart from competitors, and exactly the same for every circuit. So the speed or sprint (short race) bicycle is the most stripped-down cycling machine available. Cyclists zoom along at 60 kph (40 mph) or more in races, with top speeds on specially modified cycles of over 100 kph (60 mph).

Elbow rests
The rider rests her or his elbows on these 'shelves' with the forearms lying flat and pointing forwards to grip the handlebars above. The streamlined, torpedo-shaped ends stop the elbows slipping off sideways.

No controls
There are no brakes or gears, so the handlebars look very bare. They face forward so the rider can crouch over them, hands at the front and forearms facing forwards with elbows together. This is the best position for streamlined pedalling.

No gears
The moving parts of gear changers would add friction, weight and wear to the cycle. The sizes of the two gear wheels or cogs, front and back, are chosen by the rider at the start to suit his or her own cycling style, the track, the length of the race, the skill of the competitors and the conditions.

No brakes
There is rarely any need to brake on the special oval, banked cycle track. Brakes merely add more weight and air resistance and get in the way. The pedals can be used to slow the bike down by their fixed drive to the rear wheel.

No left fork
On a normal cycle there are two tubes on either side of the front wheel in a Y shape or fork. The sprint or speed cycle has only one, to cut down air resistance. Like other forward-facing parts it has a narrow leading edge and smooth sides for streamlining.

Not many spokes
The front wheel has three thin spokes. It does not have to be as strong as the rear wheel, which must transmit the turning force from the rear gear cog to the ground, so it can have less construction material.

HIGH GEARS
As you cycle along a level road on an ordinary bike, you push the pedals around once and the back wheel turns around about two times. But sprint and speed cycles have very high gear ratios or combinations. On a speed bike one turn of the pedals turns the back wheel around more – four, five or even more times!

SUPERBIKE

Windshield
The wind is very strong at more than 200 kph (120 mph). The windshield pushes the rushing air up and over the driver, who is also crouched down with head forward into the wind for streamlining.

Front suspension
The front forks are tubes with springs and hydraulic (oil-filled) or pneumatic (air-filled) dampers inside, to smooth out bumps in the road.

Brake calipers
The brake lever works the calipers, which press the brake pads onto the brake disc with a squeezing, scissor-like action.

Brake discs
The brake blocks or pads in the calipers press on to a large metal disc that is fixed to the road wheel and turns with it, to slow it down. The friction makes the disc hot, so it has holes in it for better cooling. Most superbikes have twin discs on the front wheel.

Few spokes
Many modern motorbikes do not have bicycle-type spokes in the wheels. The whole wheel is cast from one piece of metal alloy to make it strong but light. The lighter the wheel, the faster the engine can get it turning.

Slicks
Race tracks and fast roads are usually smooth and free of mud and dirt. So the superbike's tyres, or slicks, do not need tread. They are just plain, soft, sticky rubber to grip the tarmac.

Wraparound
The tyre surface wraps around both sides. This allows the rider to lean over at an amazing angle to balance while going round corners at great speed, with the tyre still gripping the road.

In-line twin V
This engine has two cylinders, one behind the other.

Fairings
A curved plastic or metal cover wraps around the main body of the motorbike to cut down wind resistance.

POWER, WEIGHT AND SPEED

The key to a fast vehicle is its power-to-weight ratio. This compares the weight of the vehicle with the amount of power that its engine produces to drive it along. A superbike might weigh about 170 kilograms (375 pounds) and have an engine that produces 160 horsepower. A family car weighs up to 10 times as much and has an engine that is half as powerful. So its power-to-weight ratio is 20 times less! No wonder superbikes are among the fastest of all vehicles – and so exciting to ride.

Low handlebars
The rider crouches low over the handlebars to minimize wind resistance.

Rider's seat
This is scooped out so that the driver sits as low as possible, hunched over the fuel tank for least wind resistance.

Exhaust
Exhaust gases and fumes from each cylinder flow along pipes that come together into one pipe. They pass through the silencer box before emerging into the air at the back, away from rider and passenger.

Rear suspension
The rear wheel is at the end of a long lever–like arm called a swinging or trailing arm. This pivots with the main chassis just behind the engine. Large springs and hydraulic dampers smooth out bumps and vibrations.

Chain drive
Toothed cogs (sprockets or gear wheels) and a link chain transfer turning power, from the engine between the wheels to the rear wheel. Some bikes have a spinning drive shaft instead of a chain.

Gear pedal
The rider changes gear with a foot pedal by flicking it up and down. The foot pedal on the other side applies the rear brake.

HOW MANY CCS?

A cc is a measure of volume. One cc is one cubic centimetre, that is, a cube roughly the size of a sugar lump. Motorbikes, cars and other vehicles have engines measured in ccs or litres (one litre is 1,000 ccs). The volume that's measured is the amount of air pushed aside as the pistons move their full distance inside their cylinders.

- A small moped or track motorbike is 50 ccs.
- A small racing motorcycle is up to 250 cc.
- A medium motorcycle is 500 ccs.
- A large motorcycle is 750 or 900 ccs.
- There are also superbikes of 1,000 ccs (one litre) and more!
- A smallish family car might have an engine size of 900–1,000 ccs (up to one litre).
- Big luxury cars are 2.5 litres or more.

F1 RACING CAR

Front wing
The specially shaped wing produces a force that presses the car down on to the track.

Radio aerial
The driver and his racing team can keep in contact by radio.

Tyre
F1 tyres are wide and have hardly any tread pattern. Tyres for use in the wet have more pattern. During a race, the tyres can heat up to 110 °C.

Wheel
Each wheel is held in place by a single screw-on wheelnut, which can be removed very quickly. This is so that the wheels and tyres can be changed rapidly during a race.

Steering wheel
The small steering wheel is fitted with buttons and switches that enable the driver to change gear and do many other things without having to let go of the wheel.

Cockpit
The driver's cockpit is very cramped, with almost no room to move. It is so small that the driver must remove the steering wheel before he or she gets in or out.

Sponsor's name
Running an F1 racing team is incredibly expensive. Most of the money comes from sponsors, who pay the team to advertize their names on the cars.

Fuel tanks
The tanks on either side of the driver have a honeycomb-like mesh inside. This stops the fuel slopping about too fast inside, which would upset the car's delicate balance.

Driver's survival cell
The driver lies in a tube-shaped survival cell or 'cocoon' made of extremely strong but light composite material, with only the head and arms exposed. The cell resists breaking in a crash to protect the driver.

THE CHAMPIONSHIP MACHINE

The Formula 1 racing car can accelerate from 0–160 kph (0–100 mph) and brake back to a standstill, all in less than six seconds. For this, the driver only needs first and second gears out of the six usually fitted. The fastest speeds are over 320 kph (200 mph). A Formula 1 race is usually about 300 kilometres (nearly 200 miles) and takes up to two hours. Every aspect of the car, including steering angles and fuel tank sizes, is reset for each race track. Dozens of sensors inside the car radio information on every aspect of performance back to the team in the pits. This information transfer is known as telemetry. The team can then advise the driver on the return radio link.

CARS WITH WINGS

Just as the wings of a plane lift it upwards into the air, the wings on an F1 car push it down on to the track. This is because of their shape. On a plane, the top of the wing is curved and the underside is flat, which means that the air presses less on the top than on the bottom, so the wing is pushed upward. F1 car wings are mounted the other way up, so that the force pushes them downwards. This helps the car to grip without slowing it down too much, and gives the driver more control when cornering. The wings and the body shape produce so much force that at 240 kph (150 mph) the car could race upside down on a ceiling and not fall off!

Engine
F1 engines are incredibly powerful, producing ten times the power of a normal family car engine. But they must also be as light as possible to help the car go faster.

Wing angle
The size and angle of each wing is altered to fit the type of racing circuit, depending on whether it has mainly long, fast straights or slower, twisty bends.

Back wing
Like the wing at the front, this helps to keep the car on the track – especially the rear wheels for best grip.

Exhaust manifold
The exhaust gases flow out the engine and along the exhaust pipe to the tailpipe.

Brake
As well as travelling fast, the car must be able to slow down quickly. When the driver presses the brake pedal, special pads press onto large metal discs to slow down the wheels.

TRACK STARS

Many different types of cars race around circuits. As well as Formula One (F1) there are also Formula Two, Formula Three and smaller formulas. Rally and touring cars (right) look more like normal family cars – but they too go much, much faster!

STRETCH LIMOUSINE

SUPER-LIMO

Some limousines are even longer than the one shown here. The record is the Ohrberg super-limo at 30 metres (100 feet) – the same length as a blue whale! It has 26 wheels, a king-sized water bed and a swimming pool! But it's too long to drive on most ordinary roads. It is mainly used for exhibitions and publicity events.

Intercom
Passengers can see and talk to the driver – but the driver cannot necessarily see the passengers!

Engine
A big, heavy car needs a strong, powerful engine, about 3–5 litres (3,000–5,000 cc) – that's twice as big as a family saloon. It usually takes petrol rather than diesel for quieter, smoother running.

Soft ride
The suspension is specially softened and dampened so that the ride in the limo is as smooth and comfortable as possible.

Safety button
The driver or passenger can close and lock all windows and doors using just one button. This prevents over-keen fans or curious sightseers from getting into the car.

SOS
A red alert button informs police on a special emergency radio channel in case there is a robbery or kidnap attempt on the rich or famous passengers.

THE STRETCHED PART

Originally the 'stretch' limousine was made by taking an existing luxury car, cutting it in half and welding extra panels into the gaps to make it longer. Then a new top-class interior was fitted with leather seats, deep-pile carpets and all the trimmings. Today, various specialized vehicle-makers build limos exactly to the owner's wishes. Some have fold-out beds so that they can become a luxury hotel on wheels!

Mobile office
On long journeys the limo can be a place to work. It may be fitted with a computer linked to the Internet, and a video player so that movie or music star passengers can view their latest scenes.

Radio links
Various aerials and antennae send and receive signals for radio, TV, telephone, Internet and also private encrypted (secrecy-coded) radio and walkie-talkie channels.

Tinted windows
The windows to the passenger compartment are tinted and have a reflective coating. People trying to see in from the outside can only see their own faces. The windows are often bullet-proof, too.

Comforts of home
The limo has a mobile phone, a TV (terrestrial and satellite of course), a stereo system, a courtesy bar, hot drinks and many other comforts.

Expert driver
The driver or chauffeur must be specially trained not only to drive safely and within the law, but also to start and stop very smoothly and to guide the long limo around awkward turns and avoid too-sharp corners.

Keeping cool and quiet
Air conditioning keeps passengers warm in cold weather or cool when it is hot. It also filters out the smoke and fumes from traffic jams. Special body panels and thick windows keep out the noise.

WHO BUYS A STRETCH LIMO?

Whoever wants one and has enough money! However, it is a very expensive 'toy' to leave sitting in the garage. And it may not get through the barrier at the local supermarket car park. This is why 19 out of 20 large limousines are owned by vehicle hire companies. A limo can be rented by the hour, day, week or longer. The driver costs money, too. Big limos are hired for film and music stars, bosses of big companies, royalty, presidents and prime ministers, important politicians and public figures. And also the ordinary family who decide to splash out on a special day, such as a wedding or anniversary.

4WD - FOUR WHEEL DRIVE

Silencer
This box in the exhaust pipe makes the waste gases and fumes from the engine slower and quieter. It may also contain a CAT (catalytic convertor) with special substances that remove some of the most dangerous chemicals in the fumes.

ATTs
All terrain tyres have thicker, chunkier tread than normal road tyres. They give good all-purpose grip on a variety of surfaces, from motorways to ploughed fields.

Chassis
Steel box girders make the car's chassis or framework very strong and rigid, so that it can withstand knocks from rocks and potholes.

Rear door
Some rear doors are hinged to the roof so they lift up in one piece. Others are horizontal two-part so the window section folds up and the lower solid part hinges down to form a tailgate platform. Still others are vertical two-part, hinged at each side so they open in the middle.

Rear drive
The rear drive or half shafts turn the rear road wheels when the vehicle is in RWD or 4WD mode.

Light cages
If a 4WD is used off-road it may skid and bump into trees, posts and other objects. Wire cages around the lights prevent their coverings and bulbs from being smashed. It's easier to straighten out the wire cage than to replace the bulb and cover.

Limited slip diff
This box of gear cogs stops the vehicle from getting bogged down in slippery mud.

Suspension
4WDs have strong, stiff suspension to cope with bumps and lumps on rough ground and also with the heavy loads they may carry.

Prop shaft
The propeller shaft carries the turning force from the engine back to the rear road wheels.

WHY 4WD?

A normal family car is 2WD or two wheel drive – only two of the road wheels are turned by the engine. In small cars it may be the front two (FWD), in larger ones it's the rear two (RWD). In a 4WD (four-wheel drive) vehicle all four road wheels are made to turn by the engine. This allows much more power to get through to the road, giving improved grip or traction. The vehicle has a better grip on slippery mud and ice. There is more control in going up and down very steep hills and getting out of potholes or over rocks and roots. It also allows heavier loads to be carried.

However, 4WD uses up much more fuel. This is because the engine has to turn and work an extra set of road wheel drive parts. So most 4WDs have a lever or button that switches to 2WD for smooth roads, to save fuel and wear and tear.

Head restraint
As a 4WD travels over rough ground the passengers bump and sway about. Shaped restraints help to steady their heads so that they can avoid neck pain and whiplash injuries.

Engine
Most 4WDs have diesel engines. They may be heavier and noisier than petrol engines, but they are usually more reliable and also need less servicing and maintenance.

Drive control
The driver uses a lever or shiftstick to change between FWD, RWD and 4WD.

Front drive
The front drive shafts turn the front road wheels when the vehicle is in FWD or 4WD mode.

Disc brakes
A big, heavy car like a 4WD needs strong brakes, so it is fitted with disc brakes all around. These are power-assisted, which means that the driver's pressure on the foot pedal is greatly boosted by hydraulic pressure supplied by the engine.

EVEN MORE GRIP

Four wheels turning may not be enough in very slippery conditions like ice and snow. So special snow chains are wrapped around the tyres to give even more 'purchase' (grip).

LIMITED SLIP DIFF

In a 2WD vehicle, the wheels on either side of the axle can rotate at different speeds while still being driven by the engine. This is called the diff or differential. But it can cause trouble when off road. Imagine the left back wheel of the car is in a very slippery place such as on ice. It has hardly anything to grip, so it can spin almost freely. The diff allows it to do this, while the right back wheel – which is on dry tarmac and can grip – simply stays still. The vehicle is stuck! This doesn't happen when a vehicle has limited or non-slip diff. Only a limited difference is allowed between the speeds of the two wheels. Beyond this the drive is still applied to the slower wheel, which hauls the vehicle out of the rut, so it's no longer stuck.

DIGGER

Lights
To get the job done on time the digger and driver may have to work nights. The lights move with the bucket so it is always brightly lit. There are also lights at the rear, and the driver's seat swivels round, too, since a digger spends plenty of time in reverse.

Hydraulic hoses
High-pressure oil is pumped along these flexible pipes into the cylinders to work the rams. The pipes bend so that the digger booms and bucket can move and they have steel mesh inside their walls for extra strength.

Bucket tilt rams
The bucket tilts up or down when these hydraulic rods and pistons push or pull on it.

'Artic'
The digger is articulated – it has a hinge or joint in the middle. It steers not by twisting the wheels but by moving the whole front end, including the bucket, to one side or the other.

Bucket
An average bucket is 2.5–3 metres (7 or 8 feet) wide. It is not always full of earth or rocks. The digger can be used to carry loads, such as bags of cement or blocks of bricks, around the site.

SWL
Most construction machines have SWLs, safe working loads. A digger may have a SWL of 7–8 tonnes (about 7–8 tons) for the bucket.

Main booms
These link the digger body to the bucket. They are moved by hydraulic rams.

Raise–lower rams
This pair of hydraulic rods and pistons pushes the booms and raises the bucket more than 3 metres (9 feet) into the air, so it can tip its contents into a dump truck or earthmover.

BUCKETS OF BUCKETS
The bucket shown here is a typical all-purpose design for gouging into and lifting soil, earth, small rocks, shingle, gravel and sand. There are many other bucket designs for different jobs. A smoothing bucket is lower and wider to scrape a large area level. A basket bucket is made of steel bars like a cage for lifting lighter, looser material such as hay, straw and household refuse.

Cab

The driver sits in an air-conditioned, vibration-proofed and sound-proofed cab. This protects the driver from being deafened and shaken up by a day's work.

Controls

Hand levers or buttons control the bucket's movements. Floor pedals and the steering wheel make the whole digger move about.

Engine

A heavy-duty diesel engine provides the power for turning the wheels and for the hydraulic system to raise and lower the bucket. The engine produces about 180–200 horsepower (almost three times the power of a smallish family car engine).

Massive tyres

A big digger has tyres taller than an adult person. They have deep tread to grip soft ground. Sometimes they are filled partly with water for extra weight and grip.

DIGGERS GALORE

Diggers, excavators and other load-movers find jobs in all kinds of work, from piling up scrapped cars, to scooping up gravel and sand for building, to scraping up sea salt from shallow coastal lagoons.

IT'S ALL DONE BY HYDRAULICS

Many large vehicles and machines rely on hydraulic systems. They use oil under very high pressure. It is pumped along a pipe or hose into a large metal tube-shaped cylinder. Closely fitting inside the cylinder is a rod-shaped piston. As the oil is forced into the cylinder it pushes the piston in front of it. The piston usually has a long metal rod fixed to it and the other end of the rod is linked to the part that moves. The pressure is so great that if a hose sprang a leak, the thin jet of oil spurting out of it would blast a small hole straight through the body of a person standing in the way.

Like our own muscles, hydraulic pistons can only push. For two-way movement there are two pistons that rock the part to be moved like a see-saw. Or two pistons face each other in the same long cylinder and the oil is pumped from one end of the cylinder to the other. This gives push-pull power.

MONSTER TRUCK

Cockpit
There are lots of extra dials and controls in the cab, because many running conditions of the highly tuned engine, such as temperatures and pressures, must be closely monitored. The dashboard looks more like a plane cockpit or flight deck.

Air horns
Compressed air blasts out of the multi-horns to make a sound heard more than 2 kilometres (1 mile) away.

CB radio
Drivers keep in touch with each other by CB or citizen's band radio. They chat and pass the time of day, discuss the weather and road conditions, or their trucks and loads, and warn each other of traffic jams or accidents.

Gears
There may be 10, 12 or more gears to help the truck pull away uphill with its 40-tonne load or cruise down the motorway at its maximum speed.

Driver's seat
The driver's seat is reinforced and strengthened, with a pilot-like safety harness for a seat belt, to cope with the tremendous acceleration and cornering speed.

Limiter
Working trucks are fitted with speed limiters since in many countries they are not allowed to go as fast as ordinary cars.

Engine
The giant turbocharged diesel engine may be 10 times the size of a family car engine. Some speed trucks are even fitted with jet engines as used on fighter aircraft!

Shiny chrome
On a show truck such as this many of the parts are coated with chrome metal for a shiny, hard-wearing appearance. But that means a lot of polish to keep the vehicle looking clean!

Square shape
This truck has few curves. Its design is flat-sided and squared-off. This makes it look strong and powerful. But it is not so good for speed and fuel economy.

TRUCK SHAPES

In the days before power-assisted controls, truck driving was a job for big strong people – usually men. The trucks were designed to look masculine, powerful and even menacing, with box-like shapes. However, these designs are very poor at pushing aside air smoothly. For each kilometre (just over half a mile) that a big boxy truck travels, it must push aside 20 tonnes (about 20 tons) of air. This high amount of resistance or drag uses up huge amounts of fuel. Modern trucks have more curved, streamlined shapes to save fuel.

Exhaust stack
Exhaust fumes are dangerous, even deadly if breathed in, because they contain poisonous gases such as carbon monoxide. They must be vented from an opening higher than all occupied parts of the vehicle. So this exhaust stack is about 4 metres (11 feet) high!

Sleeper
This monster truck has a small room just behind the driver's cab. It has beds, cupboards, a washbasin and a small cooker. On long journeys the driver and co-driver can rest here or pull into an overnight truck stop.

DAYS ON THE ROAD
Drivers may spend days driving a truck from coast to coast, so small personal comforts are very important.

Wheels
The enormous wheels and tyres are chest–high to an adult person. Some trucks have two pairs of front wheels, one behind the other – and both pairs turn with the steering wheel.

Artic link
The truck is designed to haul a trailer fitted with an articulated link, sometimes called the 'fifth wheel'. The front of the trailer hooks into and rests on a large metal disc at the rear of the truck itself, which is known as the tractor unit. This allows the whole vehicle to articulate or bend at the artic link.

Fuel tank
The fuel tank is of shiny chrome (on a working truck it would be dull grey or black). It holds more than 2,000 litres (140 gallons) of diesel fuel, which is 40 times as much as an ordinary car.

Electrics and hydraulics
The rear of the truck has connectors and sockets for the wires and hydraulic hoses on the trailer unit. These allow the driver to control the lights, brakes and other equipment on the trailer.

POWERED EVERYTHING

A large vehicle like this truck is so big and heavy that the steering, brakes and other features are powered or power-assisted. For example, the driver puts on the brakes by pressing the brake pedal. But the driver's leg and foot do not produce all the physical force necessary to press the brake pads on to the brake discs. Pushing the brake pedal works switches called actuators that are connected to the hydraulic system driven by the engine. The hydraulic system's oil-filled cylinders and hoses produce the great force needed to press the brake pads on to the discs.

MOUNTAIN RAILWAY

Pantograph contact
The sliding bar contact picks up electricity from the current wire. The folding arm keeps the bar in good contact with the current wire to keep the electricity flowing and reduce sparks.

Suspension cable and current wire
A strong suspension cable holds up a current wire designed to carry the electric current.

Insulator
Ceramic insulators stop electricity from leaking down the pylon into the ground. They are shaped like stacked cones so that water and ice do not build up on them, causing a short circuit.

Passenger door
Passengers enter and leave by many doors along the side of the car. This makes station stops quicker.

Snow shovels
Angled blades push loose snow off the rails and out of the way as the car moves along.

HIGHER AND CHEAPER
Mountain railways are difficult to build and maintain. The track must be fairly straight and may have to be blasted out of the steep rock. It is a constant battle to keep snow and ice off the track and the overhead power wires often ice up, too. A cheaper alternative for some regions, especially tourist resorts and winter sports centres, is the cable car. This is not affected by snow and ice on the ground. It can't work in very windy or stormy weather, but few holidaymakers are out and about in these types of conditions!

De-icer
Chemical sprays remove ice from the track and rack so the car can keep moving even in very cold conditions.

Motor
The electric motor runs on current picked up from the overhead wire. Sets or trains of gears connect it to the rack drive cog and the main wheels of the car. In some types of electric locomotives the motor can help braking by altering the way electricity flows through it, so that it resists being turned rather than causing a turning motion. This is known as rheostatic braking, and adds to the general braking system so the car does not race away downhill.

Air horns
Very loud horns blow to scare animals off the track or to alert people to the train's approach.

OVER THE SNOW
In one type of cable car the cars are fixed to the cable, which moves around in an endless loop carrying all the cars with it. In another each car has a motor and its wheels move along the stationary cable.

Two cabs
When the train reaches the stop or station at the top of the line, the driver goes to the other end of the car and gets in the cab there, to drive it back down again.

Toothed rack
A strip or rack of teeth runs along the middle of the track between the rails. These are gripped by the rack drive cog on the underside of the train for non-slip propulsion.

Inclined track
The track slants at the same angle all the way up the line. Otherwise the drive cog would not grip the rack.

Wheel cog
This gear wheel is rotated by the motor and in turn makes the main drive wheel spin around. It can also be used as part of the braking system.

Rack drive cog
The teeth of this gear wheel fit between the teeth of the track rack to haul the car up the slope.

TGV

Suspension (catenary) cable
This cable holds and supports the current wire below it. The suspension cable is made of metals designed to withstand the strain of hanging and being blown about by the wind. The current wire is less strong but made of metals able to carry or conduct electricity very well.

Current (power or trolley) wire
This carries the very high voltages of electric current picked up by the train as it passes below. The current strength may be 25,000 volts or more – 100 times the strength of normal household mains electricity.

Pylon
Tall towers made of steel or concrete beams hold up the electric power lines.

Driver's cab
The driver's display monitors the conditions in the electrical circuits, motors and other equipment. It also monitors the brakes, automatic doors and other machinery further back in the passenger cars.

Drive gear train
Gear wheels slow down the spinning motion of the traction motors and make it more powerful to turn the drive wheels of the power car.

Wheels
Railway wheels have flanges on the inside that project down on to the inner side of the rail, so the wheel does not slip off the rail.

STRAIGHT AHEAD

High-speed trains must have even straighter tracks than normal trains, with very gradual curves, or they would tip over as they went around corners.

FASTER TRAINS

Modern electric passenger trains whizz through city and countryside at tremendous speed. The French TGV (*train à grande vitesse* or very fast train) has reached 515 kph (320 mph) on a special speed run. Other high-speed services that reach 300 kph (190 mph) include Eurostar between England and Continental Europe through the Channel Tunnel, ICE in Germany and the Shinkansen or Bullet trains in Japan.

DC pantograph
In some countries the current wire carries DC or direct current. This flows in one direction. It is picked up by the pantograph.

Compressor
This produces high-pressure air to work the brakes.

AC pantograph
This pantograph picks up the AC, alternating current. This means the direction of the electricity changes to and fro many times each second, usually 50 or 60.

Inter-car bogie
Most train cars have two wheeled bogies, one at each end. This train has a bogie under the join between one car and the next. This method means fewer wheels and parts, and less weight. But the cars cannot be separated from each other.

Wheel bogie
Railway wheels are usually in sets of four, two pairs, on a trolley or chassis called a bogie. This is hinged so it can turn to the side as the train goes around a curve. It also has springs to absorb vibrations and bumps from the rails so that the passengers have a smooth ride.

Rectifiers
These electrical devices change AC into DC to work the lights, controls, hydraulics, brakes and other systems.

Transformers
Very high voltage AC is transformed or stepped down to lower voltages for the traction motors and other equipment.

Traction motors
These extremely powerful electric motors drive the wheels through a chain of gears.

Passenger car
Passengers sit in comfortable airline-type seats in a carriage that is soundproofed and air-conditioned.

LOCOMOTIVES

A train is made up of a locomotive, also known as a power car or traction unit, pulling passenger cars, goods (cargo) wagons and other units behind it. The locomotive or pulling part is powered in various ways:

• By steam power.

• A diesel locomotive or unit has a diesel engine that drives the wheels through a gearbox. It can be heard changing gear like a car.

• A diesel-electric locomotive has a diesel engine that drives an alternator or generator to make electricity, which is fed to electric motors that turn the wheels. Electric motors work well at all speeds, so a gearbox is not needed.

• An electric locomotive uses only electric motors, as in the train shown here.

JETSKI

Handlebars
The rider grips these and steers the craft with them as on a motorcycle. As the handlebars turn to one side they swivel the jet nozzle at the rear so it points to that side, making the craft veer around.

Twistgrip throttle
The handlebar grip is twisted to open the engine throttle and make the craft go faster. But there are no brakes!

Spray rail
This curved shelf-like part protects the rider from spray.

Fuel filler cover
Petrol is poured into the fuel tank through the fuel inlet under this cover.

Battery
The battery provides electricity to start the engine, as in a car or electric-start motorbike, and also for any lights that are fitted.

Engine
Most waterbikes have modified motorcycle or similar engines, with the gearing changed to suit the revolving speed of the impeller.

Exhaust
The exhaust gases are piped from the engine along the side of the craft and out at the back, safely away from rider and passenger.

Drive shaft
The turning motion of the engine spins the drive or prop (propeller) shaft, which turns the impeller at its rear end.

TRICKS AND STUNTS

The jetski lends itself to all kinds of tricky riding and exciting stunts. Experts can make the craft leap out of the water and spin around in mid air, or ride up a waterski ramp and turn a somersault. Races are held around marker buoys, often with a line of buoys close together when the rider has to slalom or zig-zag between them. In the group of manoeuvres called 'submarines' the rider makes the craft tilt nose-up, bounce into the air and then dive nose-down under the surface, still holding on. He or she can even turn while submerged and pop up some distance away.

Rider's seat
The rider stands, sits or kneels astride the front seat, depending on the design of the craft. He or she can crouch over the handlebars with knees and feet down in the footwells on either side. The rider also leans to the side to help steer the waterbike.

Passenger's seat
A passenger can kneel or sit behind the rider. As on a motorbike, the passenger usually stays still and upright, and leaves the rider to lean and balance the craft.

Passenger grab handle
The passenger holds onto these handles on either side.

Side rail
This type of waterbike has sides with side rails along the top, for protection and streamlining. Other types have open sides like a motorcycle.

Tow hitch
The craft can tow a small boat or a water-skier.

Impeller
This is a long, strong fan (similar to a propeller) that works as a high-speed water pump. It spins to suck in or impel water into the front of its pipe or tube through a wide opening on the underside of the craft. It then forces the water out rearwards through the nozzle as a fast, powerful, narrow jet.

Jet nozzle
Water from the impeller blasts out of the jet nozzle with great force and speed, pushing the craft along. The nozzle swings from side to side for steering, controlled by the handlebars.

Foot well
Rider and passenger put their legs on either side of the seat and their knees or feet in the wells along each side.

A NEW TYPE OF WATER CRAFT
Jetskis are like water skis with motorbike handles and seats, powered by a waterjet. They are also known as waterbikes or PWC, personal water craft. They were developed in the late 1960s by American motorcycle racer Clay Jacobson and the Japanese Kawasaki motorbike company. Their idea was to combine a motorbike, snowmobile and water skis into a one-person water vehicle that was fun to ride and race, and didn't cause injuries if the rider fell off. The first craft went on sale in 1973.

OFFSHORE POWERBOAT

Cockpit
The driver and co-driver sit in the cockpit with an array of dials, switches, buttons and screens in front of them. They rely on these instruments because the waves and spray mean they can often see little.

Strengthened hull
The offshore powerboat is a brutal machine. It smashes through the ocean waves at speeds of over 150 kph (90 mph). The main body or hull must be light yet extremely strong to withstand the battering, since waves at this speed are like hammer blows. The hull is usually made of aluminium or carbon fibre composite.

Spray rail
This lip or shelf along the hull pushes most of the spray and water aside so it does not break over the boat itself.

THE RACE
Powerboat races may be around a marked-out course or across the open sea from one town or island to another. This type of racing looks glamorous but it is very tiring and stressful.

SAFETY FIRST
Speeding powerboats don't lie in the water and push it aside. They plane or skim over the surface. Only the very rear parts with the screws and rudders dip into the water. However, the boat can't avoid tall waves, and these produce huge shocks as they hit. For this reason the crew must be fit and tough. The driver steers the powerboat, using satellite navigation and many other electronic aids. The co-driver controls the speed of the engines using their throttles and adjusts the boat's trim. Both crew are attached to a 'kill switch' by long cords. If they are accidentally thrown out of their seats the kill switch stops the engine so that the powerboat does not race away out of control across the sea.

F1 BOATS

Offshore powerboats have incredible strength and power for racing across the open sea. And just as Formula One is the top level for racing cars around a special track, Formula One powerboats (smaller than the boat shown here) are the top level on water. They race in sheltered waters around marker buoys, following a course similar to a Formula 1 car circuit, for 50–60 laps. They are small and streamlined catamarans – two long, slim hulls side by side under the main body. F1 boats have outboard engines, fixed on by a hinged bracket at the back. They can reach speeds of more than 250 kph (150 mph).

Aerofoil wing
The roof of the cockpit is an aerofoil wing. It helps to lift the boat's hull further out of the water for greater speed.

Ram air intake
Air for the engines is scooped in by the intakes, which are positioned away from the main spray areas.

Engine access covers
The covers lift off to reveal the engines for adjusting, maintenance, repair and refitting new engines.

Tailgate rams
The rear or tailgate of a powerboat may be hinged to the main hull. As the boat changes speed or alters its direction to the wind the front of the hull lifts up and planes (skims) by varying amounts. The angle of the tailgate automatically adjusts to keep the screws in their best position in the water.

Rudders
Twin rudders are positioned just behind the screws. This is the best position for making the boat turn sharply as it steers at speed around a buoy or small island during a race.

Gearbox
The turning speed of the engine is changed by gears into the best turning speed for the screw (propeller).

Screws
Twin screws (propellers) thrust the boat forwards.

Trim flaps
Wind, waves and currents can make the boat slew or move diagonally even when the steering wheel is set straight ahead. So it is 'trimmed' with small rudder-like flaps or tabs to counteract these forces. Trimming makes the craft travel straight ahead with the wheel in central position.

CRUISE LINER

Restaurant
Many cruise liners serve excellent food and drinks. In addition to the main restaurant there are also fast-food outlets, snack bars and cafes. You can get a meal or drink any time of day or night.

Bulkhead
A bulkhead is a wall or partition across a boat or ship from side to side. In case of accident the doors and other openings in it can be closed to make it watertight.

Patio deck
Loungers, sun chairs and tables near the restaurant and bar area are for eating, drinking, chatting and enjoying the view.

Pool deck
There's no shortage of water – the swimming pool is topped up from the sea. Of course, the water is filtered and treated with germ-killing chemicals first!

Sun deck
As the liner speeds along, the front end is very windy but the rear deck is usually sheltered. Passengers can laze here out of the breeze.

Rudder
This moveable flap steers the ship. If it swings to the left the water pushes against it and makes the rear of the liner move to the right, swinging the whole liner to the left.

Screw
As the screw or propeller turns it forces water backwards past its angled blades and so pushes the ship forwards.

Engine room
The massive diesel or gas turbine engines are deep in the rear of the liner. Their noise and vibrations are insulated or cut off from the rest of the ship. The heat from the exhaust gases is used for the ship's heating system before the gases are sent through the funnel to the open air.

THE 'BIG SHOP'

A cruise liner for about 2,000 passengers may have almost 1,000 crew to look after them and the ship. That's 3,000 people to feed and supply with drinks. The ship must take plenty of supplies in case the engines fail and it's late back to port. An average shopping list for a two-week voyage might include:

- 12 tonnes (12 tons) of potatoes, pasta and rice
- 25 tonnes (25 tons) of vegetables
- 40 tonnes (40 tons) of fresh fruit
- 25 tonnes (25 tons) of meat and fish
- 30,000 bottles of wine
- 34,000 litres (60,000 pints) of beer and lager

Radome
Radar, radio and satellite navigation equipment are protected inside a dome against wind, rain and other severe weather. The radio signals pass easily through the dome.

Bridge
The captain and crew have a good all-round view from the bridge, high up near the front of the ship.

Lifeboats
By law the lifeboats, liferafts and similar emergency equipment should have a seat or place for every person on board the ship. The crew give regular demonstrations of what do to in an accident.

Premier cabins
The luxury or executive cabins are larger and more comfortable than the economy cabins. They are higher in the ship so there are fewer stairs to climb to the public areas and they have better views from the portholes.

Indoor pool
The pool is part of the fitness suite which also has workout and gym equipment, a massage table, sunbeds and a sauna.

Cinema-theatre
Movies, videos, songs, shows, speeches, band performances, discos and other events take place in the theatre. This provides entertainment in the evenings or when the weather is poor.

Economy cabins
Smaller cabins lower in the liner have less of a view from the porthole (window). If they are interior cabins they have no view at all! This is why they cost less than the premier cabins.

THE FALL AND RISE OF THE CRUISE LINER

During the early twentieth century, when few people travelled by air, the cruise liner was very popular. It was a floating hotel that took holidaymakers to faraway places, which they visited from the liner by boarding smaller boats.

With the rise of jetliners, package holidays and car hire in the mid-twentieth century, people became more adventurous travellers. Cruise ships seemed slow and restricted. You had to go where the captain took you, and for days at a time you were stuck on board with only a limited amount to see and do.

However, the early twenty-first century has seen a revival in luxury cruising, with some of the biggest and best-equipped new ships ever. They are more like floating town centres than floating hotels. Now more than 10 million people enjoy pleasure cruises every year.

HYDROFOIL

Wheel house
This is where the controls are sited. They are a combination of those from a ship, an airplane and a car.

Wheel
As in a normal boat, the wheel makes the rudder at the rear of the craft swing from side to side for steering at low speed. It also twists the front hydrofoil and its struts from side to side for steering at high speed.

HYDROFOIL FERRIES

Around the world, hydrofoil ferries take passengers on short, fast trips. The larger ones carry 300 passengers at speeds of more than 60 kph (40 mph). Jet hydrofoils or jetfoils have water jets or turbines instead of screws. Hydrofoils are especially useful for carrying people between the mainland and nearby islands.

Bow mooring cleats
Ropes or lines from the shore are tied around these cleats when the hydrofoil comes alongside its mooring place or berth, lowering in the water as it slows down.

Hull
The hull sits in the water at low speed but rises above it into the air on the hydrofoil struts as the craft picks up speed.

BOAT ON SKIS

The hydrofoil is an underwater wing. It works in the same way as an airplane wing or aerofoil. Its shape is curved from front to back on top, and flatter from front to back on the underside. As the foil moves forwards, water must flow further over the longer curved upper surface than underneath. So water moves faster above the foil than below. This faster flow creates less pressure above the foil, with the result that the foil is sucked upwards by a force called lift. At high speed the lift is enough to raise the whole craft out of the water. This greatly reduces the water friction or drag along the hull, which slows down a normal boat. It also makes for a smoother ride. But hydrofoils cannot travel in big waves and stormy conditions.

Radar scanner

Skylights
During daylight the middle of the cabin is lit by these windows in the roof deck. They can be used as emergency exits in case of an accident.

Stern mooring cleat
The craft is moored by this cleat when it arrives at its destination.

Life belts
If someone falls into the water, a lifebelt on its rope helps the rescue.

Screw
The spinning angled blades push the water backwards and drive the craft forwards.

Engine
A diesel or gas turbine engine provides the power to turn the screw and propel the hydrofoil along. Its construction is strong and heavy since weight is less important in ships and boats than land vehicles.

Prop shaft
The shaft is spun by the engine and has the screw (propeller) at its end. On a hydrofoil the shaft is extra-long and angled down and back. This means the screw stays in the water as the craft rises with speed to 'cruising height'.

Hydrofoil
This is the name for the ski-like part underneath, and the craft was named after it. It has an aerofoil shape that creates a lifting force as it moves through the water and its depth and angle are continually adjusted by computer.

Side board
Passengers and crew can enter through the door or walk alongside the craft and on to the shore.

HI-TECH HYDROFOILS

The type of hydrofoil shown here is called a submerged-foil. The whole of each hydrofoil stays under the water. Because the foils are not as wide as the boat, there is a risk of the craft tipping over on its side. 'Pingers' along the underside of the craft beam ultrasonic clicks down on to the water surface, which reflects them back to sensors. (This system, called sound-radar or sonar, is also used to measure the depth of the sea-bed, and by bats to fly in the dark.) The on-board computer continually measures the height of the craft and its angle or tilt from front to back and side to side. It then adjusts the angle or tilt of the foils so the craft stays steady and safe.

SUPERTANKER

THE GIANT IN PORT

Supertankers are so vast and awkward to manoeuvre that they do not come into small harbours. Large terminals are built for them where there is plenty of room and the water is deeper. Small, powerful tug boats push them into position.

Crew gangway
Crew members can quickly reach any part of the deck along the gangways. Often they use bicycles, since the whole ship may be more than 300 metres (800 feet) long.

Pipes
A maze of pipes connects the various tanks and pumps with the connectors for loading or unloading the oil.

Pumps
Various pumps force the oil into the tanks when loading at the oil production platform. They suck it out again when the supertanker reaches its destination – the oil refinery or storage depot.

Mooring winches
Thick cables or hawsers are used to moor the ship against its platform or terminal. They are pulled in by powerful winches and stored below deck on the voyage.

NEDLLOYD ROUEN

Anchor
The huge anchor is lowered to the sea-bed when the supertanker needs to stay in the same place but cannot moor or tie up. The thrusters and main screws may also be used to keep the ship still or 'on station'.

Thrusters
These small propellers or screws in the side of the hull make the boat swing sideways to help with steering.

Valves
The oil is pumped on and off through connectors. Valves inside make sure it flows the correct way.

SAFETY AND POLLUTION

The supertanker may be gigantic, yet it floats easily. Oil is lighter than water and floats on top of it. However, this can cause great problems. A supertanker accident may release vast quantities of thick crude oil that floats on the sea as slicks. It kills fish, sea birds and other marine life. If it washes ashore it can devastate coastal regions and destroy seashore wildlife. Newer tankers have hulls with double skins to prevent them leaking oil in an accident, and very strict fire precautions.

Satellite and radio links
The ship is in direct contact with several types of satellites. They include telecom satellites for telephone, television and computer links, the GPS (global positioning system) for satellite navigation, and specialist marine satellites that provide detailed weather reports or emergency channels in case of an accident.

Funnel
Exhaust gases from the engines blow up the funnel and away into the air.

Crew quarters
When not on duty the crew live, rest, sleep and eat here.

Cargo crane
A small crane helps to lift specialist equipment, food and other supplies on and off the ship.

Bridge
This is the control centre for the ship. The captain, navigator and other senior crew have a high, clear, all-round view of the ship and its surroundings through the large windows.

Engines and screws
The engines are at the rear of the ship, separated from the oil for safety. The ship is pushed forward by one or more screws at the rear or stern.

Oil tanks
Oil is stored in many separate tanks that take up most of the ship. If a storm caused oil to slosh about in one huge tank, it might make the ship tip over or capsize.

GIANTS OF THE SEAS

Crude oil is used to make fuels such as petrol, diesel, kerosene and paraffin, also tars and bitumen for roads, and paints and pigments, plastics, mineral rubber and hundreds of other substances. Many oil reserves are under the sea-bed. Ocean drilling platforms bore holes down to harvest the crude oil. A supertanker takes it on board and carries it to an oil terminal where there are storage tanks and refineries for treatment. Supertankers are the biggest ships on the seas. Some weigh over 300,000 tonnes (294,000 tons), and are more than 300 metres (800 feet) long. They take 3–5 kilometres (2–3 miles) to steer around a corner and 5–10 kilometres (3–6 miles) to stop. They are sometimes called ULCCs, ultra large crude carriers.

Index